SCATALOG

A Kid's Field Guide to Animal Poop

HOW TO TRACK A LION

Dory Zane

"BECAUSE EVERYBODY POOPS"

WINDMILL
BOOKS

New York

To Chris, who valiantly scoops our little lions' boxes

Published in 2014 by Windmill Books, An Imprint of Rosen Publishing
29 East 21st Street, New York, NY 10010

First Edition

Editor: Amelie von Zumbusch
Photo Research: Katie Stryker
Book Design: Colleen Bialecki

Photo Credits: Cover (top) Maggy Meyer/Shutterstock.com; cover (bottom), p. 19 (right) Daniel Vesterskov/Flickr; background Kao/Shutterstock.com; p. 4 Dave Pusey/Shutterstock.com; pp. 5, 19 (left) Annie Spencer/Flickr; p. 7 Josef Friedhuber/E+/Getty Images; p. 8 JR Webb/Flickr; p. 9 Jo Crebbin/Shutterstock.com; p. 10 EastVillage Images/Shutterstock.com; pp. 11, 14, 15 iStockphoto/Thinkstock; p. 13 2630ben/Shutterstock.com; p. 17 Ken Zaremba/Flickr; p. 18 Steve Noakes/Shutterstock.com; p. 21 Natursports/Shutterstock.com; p. 22 Anup Shah/Photodisc/Thinkstock.

Library of Congress Cataloging-in-Publication Data

Zane, Dory, author.
  How to track a lion / by Dory Zane. — First edition.
      pages cm. — (The scatalog—a kid's field guide to animal poop)
  Includes index.
  ISBN 978-1-61533-884-9 (library binding) — ISBN 978-1-61533-890-0 (pbk.) —
ISBN 978-1-61533-896-2 (6-pack)
  1. Lion—Juvenile literature. 2. Animal droppings—Juvenile literature. I. Title.
  QL737.C23Z367 2014
  599.757—dc23
                                     2013019821

Manufactured in the United States of America

CPSIA Compliance Information: Batch #BW14WM: For Further Information contact Windmill Books, New York, New York at 1-866-478-0556

CONTENTS

TRACKING WITH POOP

Lions are part of the cat family. These powerful hunters are famous for their roar. If you wanted to track a lion in the wild, how would you do it? Would you look for its paw prints? Would you listen for roaring? There are many ways to track lions. One of the best is to look for their poop!

Here, a mother lion watches over her babies. Female lions are called lionesses, while babies are called cubs.

Lion poop tends to be dark colored. The large amount of blood in lions' diets is what makes their poop dark.

You can learn a lot about lions by tracking their poop. Lion poop shows where a lion has been and what it has eaten. It can tell a tracker if a lion is male or female. Poop even helps trackers guess how many lions are living in one place.

If you want to track lions, Africa is the best place to start your search. Though a small number of lions live in India's Gir Forest, Africa is home to most of the world's lions.

The savanna this lion is on is part of the Maasai Mara National Reserve, in Kenya.

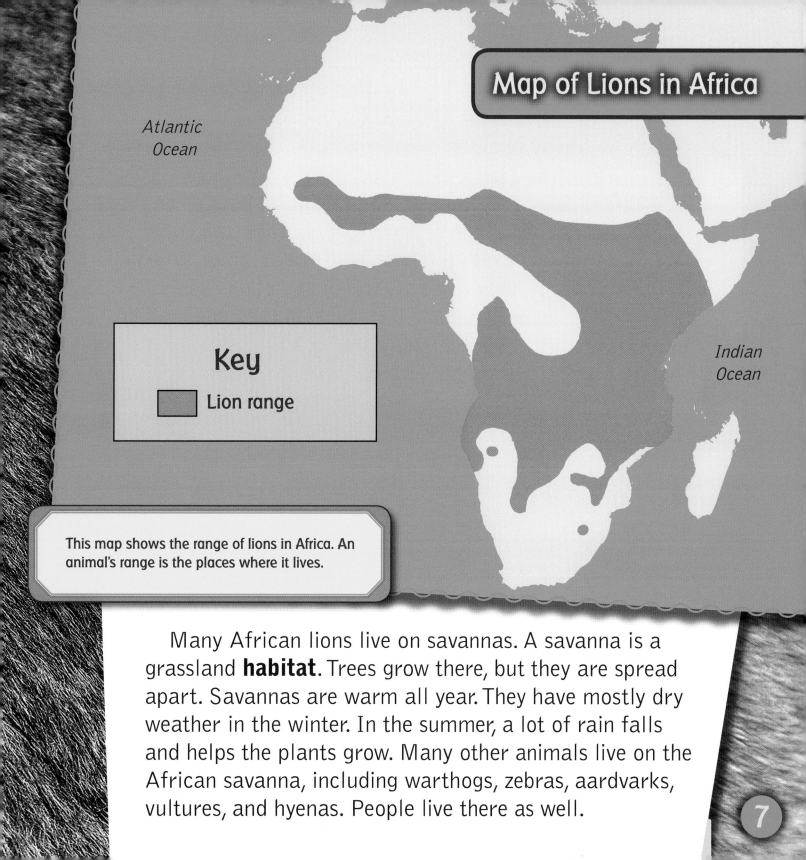

Map of Lions in Africa

Atlantic
Ocean

Indian
Ocean

Key

Lion range

This map shows the range of lions in Africa. An animal's range is the places where it lives.

Many African lions live on savannas. A savanna is a grassland **habitat**. Trees grow there, but they are spread apart. Savannas are warm all year. They have mostly dry weather in the winter. In the summer, a lot of rain falls and helps the plants grow. Many other animals live on the African savanna, including warthogs, zebras, aardvarks, vultures, and hyenas. People live there as well.

Lion trackers need to be able to recognize lions when they see them. Lions can be hard to spot. Their tan coats help them blend in with the grasses of the savanna. When trackers do spot lions, it is easy to tell male lions apart from female lions. Only male lions have **manes**. Manes help male lions look larger than they are.

A lion's muscular legs make it easy for the animal to squat while pooping!

No claw marks

Four toes

Lion tracks are a great way to track lions. Lion tracks tend to be 3.5 to 5.9 inches (9–15 cm) long. Males tend to have slightly larger tracks than females do.

Three lobes at the back

All lions have muscular bodies, powerful jaws, and sharp teeth. They have sharp claws that they can retract, or draw back into their claws. This is why you rarely see claw marks in lion tracks, or footprints.

FINDING A PRIDE

Tracking a lion might lead you to a whole group of lions. Lions are the only **social** cats. They live in groups called prides. A pride is made up of lionesses and their babies, with a few adult males. All of the lionesses in a pride are related. A small pride may have only two lionesses. A large pride may have six. Prides have a close social bond. They do not like to take in strangers.

Lionesses generally stay with their mother's pride for life. Young male lions are generally chased away at about two years old.

Male and female lions roar to **communicate** with other lions. Roaring tells other lions where a lion is. A lion's roar can be heard from more than 5 miles (8 km) away!

Lions mark their pride's territory by roaring and urinating, or peeing. An animal's territory is the land it uses and will defend against other animals of the same kind.

LEARNING TO BE A LION

Sometimes, trackers get a chance to see lion cubs. Lionesses may have between two and six cubs in a litter. The cubs are born in a den away from other lions. They weigh only 3 pounds (1 kg) at birth!

A lioness brings her cubs back to her pride when they are around two months old. While the lionesses hunt, the adult males watch the cubs. Adult lions play and wrestle with the cubs. This helps the cubs learn how to chase and pounce. At around 11 months old, the cubs join their first hunt.

Lion cubs produce smaller poop than adult lions do. In fact, lion cub poop looks a lot like the poop of other African cats. This makes it harder to identify than adult lion poop is.

CATCHING THEIR PREY

Lionesses do most of a pride's hunting. They are smaller and lighter than males, which makes them faster runners. A lioness can run the length of a football field in just 6 seconds! Lionesses are also **agile**, which means they can change directions quickly. Lionesses hunt at night and in the early morning.

Meat eaters, such as lions, have solid poop with bits of fur and bone in it. Plant eaters, such as zebras, tend to produce looser poop that has plant pieces in it.

These lionesses are getting ready to hunt. Though females do most of the hunting, males almost always eat first.

Lionesses work together to hunt **prey**. Smaller lionesses chase the prey into the center of the hunting group. Then, the larger lionesses jump out and catch the prey. Lionesses bite down on the necks of larger animals to kill them. They use their sharp claws to kill smaller animals.

WHAT DO LIONS EAT?

Lions are **carnivores**. They eat only animals. Lions hunt antelope, zebras, wildebeests, elephants, rhinos, and crocodiles. They also steal prey from other predators, such as leopards, cheetahs, and hyenas. Lions even sometimes eat dead animals that have started rotting!

LION DIGESTIVE SYSTEM

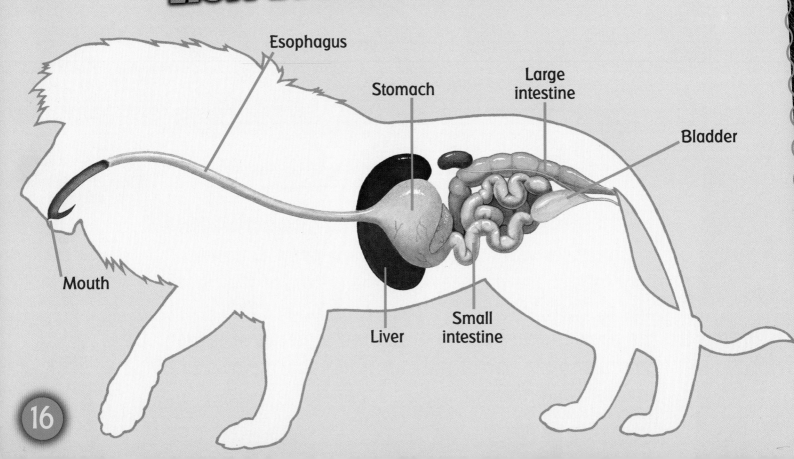

Esophagus

Stomach

Large intestine

Bladder

Mouth

Liver

Small intestine

Segments

Pointed at one end

Bit of bone

Hairs

LION POOP

Lions **digest** their food quickly. This lets them eat a lot of food in a short time. Food passes through the lion's digestive system, making waste that leaves the body as poop. Lion poop is large and **segmented**. It is dark in color and about 1.5 inches (4 cm) thick. In lion poop, you can see fur and pieces of bone from the animals that lions eat!

CLUES FROM POOP

It can be hard to find lion poop in the wild. This is because other animals love to eat it! Lion poop is very meaty. It is a good source of food for **scavengers** such as hyenas. Trackers sometimes use dogs to help them track lion poop. Dogs sniff out poop with their powerful noses.

Scientists also track lions in other ways, such as by using radio collars. Radio collars can tell scientists where a lion is, even if they cannot see it.

LION POOP FRESHNESS CHART

FRESH POOP

- Is damp
- Is dark
- Is smelly

OLDER POOP

- Dries out
- May whiten with age
- Will not smell as much

This chart compares fresh and older lion poop. Knowing how old poop is helps trackers figure out how recently a lion passed through an area.

Scientists study lion poop, too. Some study **molecules** called DNA in lion poop. DNA is special to each animal, like a fingerprint. Looking for DNA in lion poop helps scientists track specific lions in a pride. It can also show how these lions are related to one another.

KEEPING LIONS SAFE

Lions are not in danger of dying out very soon. However, their numbers have grown much smaller over time. Scientists think there may be between 20,000 and 40,000 lions left in Africa. People have killed many lions. This is because people are afraid of lions since sometimes lions kill people. Lions kill and eat **livestock** raised by people as well. Lion habitats are also being used by people for homes or farms.

Today, many lions live in national parks or wildlife **preserves**. These lands are set aside for wild animals to use. They are great places to track lions and other animals.

Safaris let people see lions and other African animals in their natural habitats. People on safaris often ride in heavy cars to protect them from the dangerous animals they see.

USEFUL POOP

Using poop to track lions has helped us learn a lot about them. However, people also use lion poop in other ways. Domestic cats, such as house cats or stray cats, can sense that lion poop is from a bigger, stronger cat. People spread lion poop in their gardens because the smell of it keeps domestic cats out!

Poop from carnivores, such as lions, is often called scat. It tends to be smellier than plant-eaters' poop. Despite its smell, it is a great source of information!

Lions spend most of their day sleeping or resting. This gives them plenty of time to digest their food.

GLOSSARY

agile (A-jul) Able to move easily and gracefully.

carnivores (KAHR-neh-vorz) Animals that eat only other animals.

communicate (kuh-MYOO-nih-kayt) To share facts or feelings.

digest (dy-JEST) To break down food so that the body can use it.

habitat (HA-buh-tat) The kind of land where an animal or a plant naturally lives.

livestock (LYV-stok) Animals raised by people.

manes (MAYNZ) Long hair on the necks of certain animals.

molecules (MAH-lih-kyoolz) The smallest bits of matter possible before they can be broken down into their basic parts.

preserves (prih-ZURVZ) Areas set aside for the protection of plants and animals.

prey (PRAY) An animal that is hunted by another animal for food.

scavengers (SKA-ven-jurz) Animals that eat dead things.

segmented (SEG-men-ted) Having many smaller pieces.

social (SOH-shul) Living together in a group.

INDEX

A
Africa, 6, 20

B
babies, 10
bodies, 9, 17

C
carnivores, 16, 22
cat(s), 10, 22
cubs, 12

F
food, 17–18

G
group(s), 10, 15

H
habitat(s), 7, 20
hunters, 4
hyenas, 7, 16, 18

L
lioness(es), 10, 12, 14–15

M
males, 10, 12, 14

N
night, 14

P
people, 7, 20, 22
prey, 15–16

R
roar, 4, 11

S
savanna(s), 7–8

T
tracker(s), 5, 8, 12, 18

W
wild, 4, 18
winter, 7

Z
zebras, 7, 16

WEBSITES